Homes around the world

Village Homes

Nicola Barber

Crabtree Publishing Company
www.crabtreebooks.com

Crabtree Publishing Company

www.crabtreebooks.com

Editors: Hayley Leach, Ellen Rodger, Michael Hodge
Senior Design Manager: Rosamund Saunders
Designer: Elaine Wilkinson
Geography consultant: Ruth Jenkins

Photo credits: Mark Boulton/Alamy p. 20; Peter Bowater/Alamy p. 22; Dennis Cox/Alamy p. 10; Danita Delimont/Alamy title page and p. 13; GreekStockOne/Alamy p. 16, p. 27; Peter Horree/Alamy p. 7; J Marshall – Tribaleye Images/Alamy p. 25; Jeff Morgan/Alamy p. 24; nagelstock.com/Alamy p. 6; qaphotos.com/Alamy p. 18; Keren Su/China Span/Alamy p. 14; Janine Wiedel Photolibrary/Alamy p. 23; Chris Lisle/Corbis p. 15; Allison Wright/Corbis p. 12, p. 26; Bruce Harber/Ecoscene p. 19; Glen Allison/Getty p. 8; Dean Conger/Getty p. 17; Sergio Pitamitz/Getty cover and p. 11; Lonely Planet Images p. 9, p. 21.

Cover: The village of Roquebrune in France.

Title page: Over 1,000 people live in the beautiful village of Strafford, Vermont.

Activity & illustrations: Shakespeare Squared pp. 28, 29.

Library and Archives Canada Cataloguing in Publication

Barber, Nicola
    Village homes / Nicola Barber.

(Homes around the world)
Includes index.
ISBN 978-0-7787-3546-5 (bound).--ISBN 978-0-7787-3558-8 (pbk.)

    1. Housing, Rural--Juvenile literature. 2. Dwellings--Juvenile literature. 3. Villages--Juvenile literature. I. Title. II. Series: Barber, Nicola. Homes around the world.

GN395.B373 2007   j392.3'6091734   C2007-904708-4

Library of Congress Cataloging-in-Publication Data

Barber, Nicola.
    Village homes / Nicola Barber.
        p. cm. -- (Homes around the world)
    Includes index.
    ISBN-13: 978-0-7787-3546-5 (rlb)
    ISBN-10: 0-7787-3546-X (rlb)
    ISBN-13: 978-0-7787-3558-8 (pb)
    ISBN-10: 0-7787-3558-3 (pb)
    1. Dwellings--Juvenile literature. 2. Villages--Juvenile literature. 3. Country life--Juvenile literature. I. Title. II. Series.

GT172.B38 2008
392.3'6--dc22   2007030185

Crabtree Publishing Company

www.crabtreebooks.com   1-800-387-7650

Published in Canada
Crabtree Publishing
616 Welland Ave.
St. Catharines, Ontario
L2M 5V6

Published in the United States
Crabtree Publishing
PMB16A
350 Fifth Ave., Suite 3308
New York, NY 10118

Contents

Words in **bold** can be found in the glossary on page 30

What is a village home?

A village is a small group of homes and other buildings. The buildings found in a village may include a church, a few small shops, a school, and a village **hall**.

▼ Godshill is a village on the Isle of Wight, England. The roofs of homes there are made from **thatch**.

People who live in small villages often know each other. Meetings, activities, and **festivals** take place in the village hall. Some villages are near big towns or cities. Others can be far from anywhere.

▲ *The houses in this village in Sumatra have roofs made from* **corrugated iron**.

Life in a village

People like village life because it is not as busy or crowded as life in a city is. Many villages lie in beautiful **countrysides**. Villages are smaller and they are often more peaceful than towns and cities are.

▼ *Over 1,000 people live in the beautiful village of Strafford, Vermont.*

In some places, village life can be difficult. In poor villages, most people do not have much money. People may leave their villages to earn more money in the cities. They hope that life will be better there.

▲ *This family lives in a village near Quito, Ecuador, in South America.*

Underground and hilltop homes

In some villages, people use the land around them to build their homes. Cave homes can be made by digging down under the ground or by digging into cliffs.

Village life
About 40 million people live in cave homes in China today.

▲ You can see the doors and windows of these homes built into cliffs in Shanxi province, China.

Villages may be built on hilltops or steep hillsides. The homes in this village are crowded on the hilltop. The homes are close together with narrow streets between them.

▲ *The village of Roquebrune is in France. **Tiles** cover the roofs of the houses.*

Building a village home

People often use **materials** from nearby to build their village homes. Wood, stone, mud, or even animal skins are often used for the walls. Palm leaves are woven together to make some roofs.

▼ *This house is in Peru. Wooden **stilts** raise it off of the ground and keep it cool.*

The Masai people live in Kenya and Tanzania in Africa. To make their houses, the Masai stick poles into the ground. Then they **weave** a **frame** with thin branches around the poles. They cover the frame with cow dung and leave it to dry.

Village life
The smell of the dried dung helps keep insects away from a Masai house.

▲ *This woman is gathering wood in a Masai village. The Masai women usually build their houses.*

Inside a village home

Around the world, people decorate the insides of their village homes in very different ways. This couple live in a village in Rajasthan, in northwest India. They have used a blue **dye**, called **indigo**, to decorate the walls of their home.

▼ The blue dye on the walls of this house comes from the indigo plant grown in Rajasthan, India.

This house is in the village of Zalipie in Poland. The women of the village paint their houses with beautiful flower patterns. Every year, there is a competition to see who can paint the best decorations.

▲ People come from all over Poland to see the decorated homes of Zalipie village.

The weather

In villages where the weather is hot, people sometimes paint their houses white. Sunshine bounces off the white walls, keeping the insides of the houses cool.

▼ *These village homes are on the island of Mykonos, Greece.*

In cold places, people try to keep their houses warm. Thick walls made from stone or wood help keep houses warm even when it is cold and snowing outside.

▲ *Wood or coal fires help keep these homes warm in the winter in Artybash, Siberia, Russia.*

The environment

Some villages do not have a supply of clean water. Every day, people walk from villages to fetch water from far away. The water is needed for drinking and cooking, as well as washing.

▼ *These women in South Africa are drawing clean water. One pumps and the other collects the water.*

In an **ecovillage**, people try to produce all of the **energy** and food that they need. A windmill can be used to make electricity. Animals such as sheep, goats, and hens can be kept for milk and eggs.

Village life

In Africa, some women walk 10 miles (16 km) every day to find clean water.

▲ *These homes in Torup ecovillage in Denmark are made from* **recycled** *materials.*

School and play

Many villages have their own small schools, which may only have a few pupils. Some villages do not have a school at all. Children may have to travel to the nearest town or city to go to school.

▼ *In this school in Boravali, India, the children sit on the floor to do their work.*

Children in a village often go to school together and play together. Many villages have playgrounds where children run around and have fun.

▲ *These children are playing a ball game in their village in Laos.*

Going to work

Many people live in village sand travel to the nearest town or city to go to work. They may have to travel a long way every day. Other people can do their work at home, using a computer.

▼ *This man runs his business from home in a village in France. He can go to work in his backyard!*

22

Farmers often live in villages. They grow food for their families to eat. If they can, they also grow **crops** to sell at the **local** market. Some farmers keep animals, too.

▲ *This farmer is picking mandarin oranges in the village of Akyaka, Turkey.*

Getting around

Villages can be far away from the nearest town or city. Many do not have a railway line, and often there are few buses that go to the village. Cars are a popular way to get around.

▼ *This van is picking up mail from Llangwyryfon, Wales. It also takes people from village to village.*

In some parts of the world, the roads between villages are very uneven and difficult to use. People walk or travel in carts to get around. They often use animals, such as camels or **mules**, to carry their goods.

Village life

In some villages, people share taxis and car journeys to help each other travel around.

▲ *In Myanmar, a country in southeast Asia, cattle are used to pull carts.*

Where in the world?

Some of the places mentioned in this book have been labeled here.

Look at the two different pictures on this map.

- How are the homes different from each other?

- What is each home made of?

- Look at their walls, roofs, windows, and doors.

- How are these homes different from where you live?

- How are they the same?

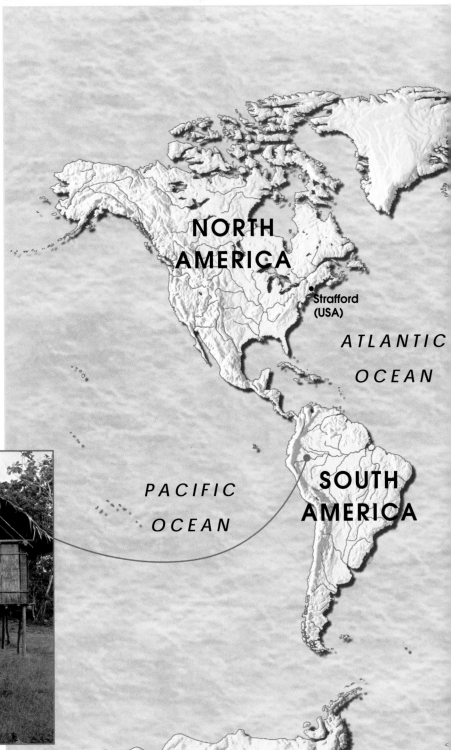

NORTH AMERICA

Strafford (USA)

ATLANTIC OCEAN

PACIFIC OCEAN

SOUTH AMERICA

*Village in the Amazon **basin**, Peru*

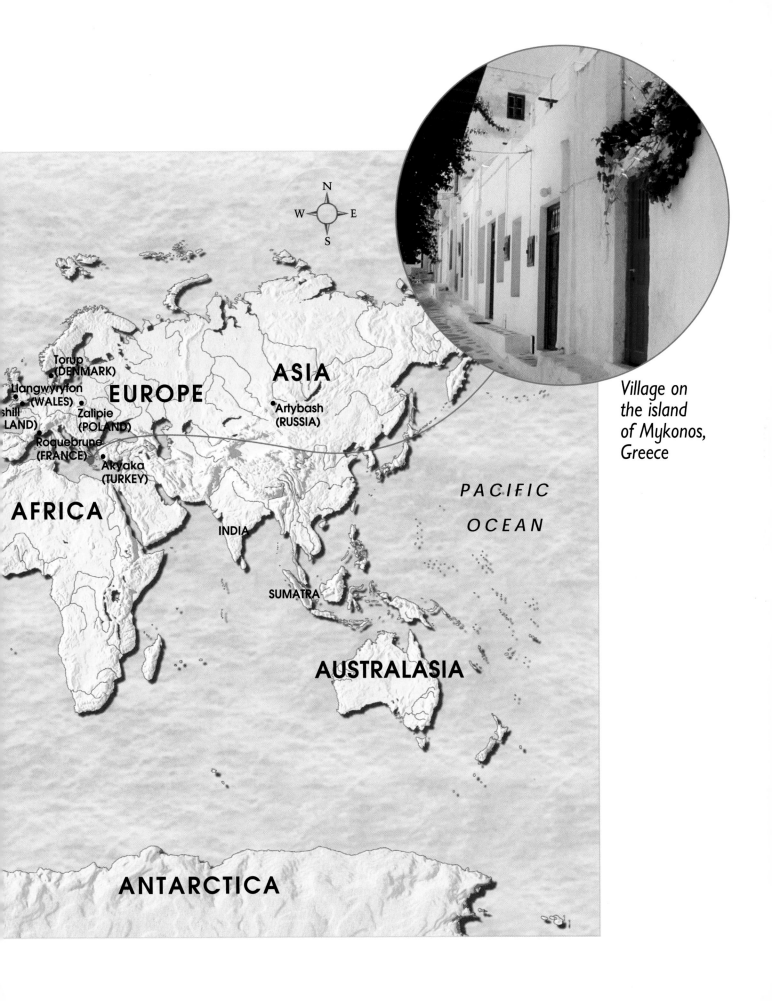

Village on the island of Mykonos, Greece

Torup
(DENMARK)

Llangwyryfon
(WALES)

shill
LAND)

Zalipie
(POLAND)

Roquebrune
(FRANCE)

Akyaka
(TURKEY)

EUROPE

ASIA

Artybash
(RUSSIA)

AFRICA

INDIA

SUMATRA

PACIFIC

OCEAN

AUSTRALASIA

ANTARCTICA

N
W E
S

Village home memory game

Play this game to help you remember the different village homes. You can play with two or more people.

What you need
- paper
- pencil
- scissors

1. Divide a sheet of paper into four rows and four columns. This should give you 16 rectangles.

2. Cut along the lines in the paper. When you finish, you will have 16 separate rectangles. These will be your game cards. Separate the cards into two piles of eight.

3. Take one pile of cards, and write one place name on each card.

Place Names

Sumatra	France	China	Russia
Peru	Poland	Kenya	Greece

4. Take the other pile of cards, and write one description on each card.

Descriptions

homes with iron roofs   homes with tile roofs

homes built into cliffs   homes on wooden stilts

homes made of branches and cow dung

homes with painted decorations

homes painted white to keep them cool

homes with thick stone walls to keep them warm

How to play the game:

Shuffle the 16 cards, and then spread them face-down on a table. Players take turns choosing two cards. If one card reads a place name and the other reads its correct description, you have a match. If not, turn the cards over again. Then have the next player take a turn. Continue to play until all cards have been matched. The player with the most matches wins!

Glossary

basin	The huge area drained by a river
corrugated iron	A sheet of iron that has ridges running along it
countryside	Wide open spaces that are not in a town or city, such as fields or farmland
crops	Plants grown for food or to sell
dye	A substance that gives color to things
ecovillage	A village where people try to produce all of their own energy, grow their own food, and be self-sufficient
energy	You need energy to make things work. Electricity is a kind of energy.
festival	A time of celebration
frame	A structure that gives something shape and strength
hall	A large room
indigo	A blue dye that comes from the indigo plant
local	Near home
material	What something is made from
mule	A cross between a donkey and a horse
recycled	Describes an item that is made from something that has already been used and is no longer needed
stilts	Poles that are used to raise something off of the ground
tile	A thin slab made from hard material. Tiles are laid in rows to cover roofs, floors, or walls.
thatch	A roof covering made from straw
weave	To thread in and out

Further information

Crabtree books to read

Early Village Life, from the Early Settler Life series
Medieval Towns, Trade, and Travel, from the Medieval World series
Life in a Longhouse Village, from the Native Nations of North America series
Colonial Home, from the Historic Communities series
Homes of the West, from the Life in the Old West series
The Lands, Peoples, and Cultures series
Homes, from The Discovering World Cultures series

Websites

http://depts.washington.edu/chinaciv/home/3intrhme.htm#variation
About homes in China

http://indahnesia.com/indonesia/SUTHOU/batak_houses.php
About homes in Indonesia

http://archilibre.org/ENG/inspiration/zalipie.html
For more pictures of Zalipie

http://www.photo-gallery.dk/oversigt/lokaliteter/torup/preview_1of8.html
For more pictures of the Torup ecovillage

Index

All of the numbers in **bold** refer to photographs.

Printed in the USA